FACTS
~ ABOUT ~
~ PRECIOUS ~
STONES

THEODORE A. KOHN & SON
— JEWELERS —

British Library Cataloguing-in-Publication Data
A catalogue record for this book is available from
the British Library

Introduction to Gemmology

Gemmology is the science dealing with natural and artificial gems and gemstones. It is considered a geoscience and a branch of mineralogy. Although some practice gemmology as a sole profession, often jewellers become academically trained gemmologists, qualified to identify and evaluate gems. Rudimentary education in gemmology for jewellers and gemmologists began in the nineteenth century, but the first qualifications were instigated after the 'National Association of Goldsmiths of Great Britain' (NAG), set up a Gemmological Committee for this purpose in 1908. This committee matured into the 'Gemmological Association of Great Britain' (also known as Gem-A), now an educational charity and accredited awarding body, with its courses taught worldwide. The first US graduate of Gem-A's Diploma Course, in 1929, was Robert Shipley who later established both the 'Gemmological Institute of America' and the 'American Gem Society'. There are now several professional schools and associations of gemmologists and certification programs around the world.

The first gemmological laboratory serving the jewellery trade was established in London in 1925, prompted by the influx of the newly developed 'cultured pearl' and advances in the synthesis of rubies and sapphires. There are now numerous Gem Labs around the world requiring ever more advanced equipment and experience to identify the new challenges - such as treatments to gems, new synthetics and other new materials. Gemstones are basically categorized based on of their crystal structure, specific gravity, refractive index and other optical properties such as pleochroism. The physical property of 'hardness' is defined by the non-linear 'Mohs Scale' of mineral hardness. Gemmologists study these factors while valuing or appraising cut and polished gemstones. Gemmological microscopic study of the internal structure is used to determine whether a gem is synthetic or natural, by revealing natural fluid inclusions and partially melted exogenous crystals, in order to demonstrate evidence of heat treatment to enhance colour. The spectroscopic analysis of cut gemstones also allows a gemmologist to understand the atomic structure and identify its origin; a major factor in valuing a gemstone. For example, a ruby from Burma will have definite internal and optical activity variance as compared to a Thai ruby.

Gem identification is basically a process of elimination. Gemstones of similar colour undergo non-destructive optical testing until there is only one possible identity. Any single test is indicative, only. For example, the specific gravity of ruby is 4.00, glass is 3.15-4.20, and cubic zirconia is 5.6-5.9. So, one can easily tell the difference between cubic zirconia and the other two; however, there is overlap between ruby and glass. And, as with all naturally occurring materials, no two gems are identical. The geological environment in which they are created influences the overall process, so that although the basics can be identified, the presence of chemical 'impurities' and substitutions along with structural imperfections vary - thus creating 'individuals.' Having said this, the three main methods of testing gems are highly successful in proper identification. These are:

- Identification by refractive index - This test determines the gems identity by measuring the refraction of light in the gem. Every material has a critical angle, at which point light is reflected back internally. This can be measured and thus used to determine the gem's identity. Typically, this is measured using a refractometer, although it is possible to measure it using a microscope.

- Identification by specific gravity – This method, also known as 'relative density', varies depending upon the chemical composition and crystal structure type. Heavy liquids with a known specific gravity are used to test loose gemstones. Specific gravity is measured by comparing the weight of the gem in air with the weight of the gem suspended in water.

- Identification by spectroscopy – This technique uses a similar principle to how a prism works, to separate white light into its component colours. A gemmological spectroscope is utilised to analyse the selective absorption of light in the

gem material. Essentially, when light passes from one medium to another, it bends. Blue light bends more than red light. Depending on the gem material, it will adjust how much this light bends. Colouring agents or chromophores show bands in the spectroscope and indicate which element is responsible for the gem's colour.

THE object of this little book may be stated in a few words.

We desire to place in the hands of our customers, in compact form, a few important facts regarding precious stones with the rules which should govern their wise selection. Larger works on this subject may be found in libraries, but the coveted hints are usually buried in scientific matter, and the size of the volume is out of all proportion to the needs of the reader who wishes to be guided in purchasing, rather than instructed in historical or technical lore.

When it is considered that there is scarcely a home where jewels of one sort or another—all representing a moneyed value—are not to be found, the subject assumes an immediate importance. It must be remembered that there is always a double argument for the accumulation of precious stones: first, their decorative, and secondly, their permanent value. On the one hand they are objects of beauty, of sentiment, and of genuine pleasure both to wearer and beholder. But on the other hand they are never to be regarded otherwise than in the light of a simple investment. From their extreme portability and absolute value (with but slight fluctuation), they are properly classed by many conservative persons with government bonds. The interest on the investment is the pleasure of their possession and use; it is as if the interest was spent semi-annually for dress or other entertainment. The investment, however, as such, is in reality more safe than a Government bond, for in times of revolution or political trouble—the times when values are most disturbed—jewels (as a form of portable and certain wealth) have always risen in price. Thus in Paris during the French Revolution, diamonds doubled in value. Many a safe investor to-day makes a practice of keeping jewels in his family in case of financial emergency, in view of the extreme uncertainty of business operations.

It seems almost unnecessary to state that jewels should never be purchased of unknown parties, and it is equally important that all such transactions should be conducted only with a firm of the very highest reputation for business integrity.

The integrity of the dealer, however, fully established, his judgment is an important matter. This must be based on long experience, close observation, and an intimate knowledge of every detail of the subject carefully revised to date. These are essentials which are of the utmost importance to the purchaser in many instances. For example, the price of colored stones and pearls is removed from the common category and only accurate judgment can safely dictate their worth; the rarity of a gem is always a factor in its price of which only the expert can properly judge.

Emerson's maxim is in point here:— "He who would bring back the wealth of the Indies must take with him the wealth of the Indies." You cannot secure value without cost.

With these general remarks let us pass to the consideration of the precious stones separately in more detail,

classifying them under three heads:—
(a) diamonds; (b) rubies, emeralds, sapphires and other colored stones: (c) pearls.

THE DIAMOND

This gem, surpassing all others in brilliancy, is found in all colors—white, yellow, orange, red, pink, brown, green, blue, black and opalescent. The light yellow and brown hues are comparatively common; the decided colors are extremely rare; only one deep-red diamond has ever been found. The colors most in demand are perfect white, bluish white, and deep golden yellow.

The diamond is simply a crystal of pure carbon, and as such is safe from all injury by acids or alkalis, and is infusible.

Diamonds formerly came in large numbers from India, later from Brazil, and now come chiefly from South Africa.

The brilliancy of a diamond depends very much upon its cutting. The most desirable form of cutting is the "brilliant," which with many modifications as to size and proportion is in general a shape as of two pyramids united at their bases, the upper one having a large plane surface, and the lower terminating almost in a point. The line of division is called the "girdle." The best proportion is when the "culet" or lower table (below the girdle) is exactly twice as deep as the "crown" or table (above the girdle). The number of "facets," or faces, varies, but in the most perfect cutting there are 58; a general average is from 42 to 74 facets. The "brilliant" is a very recent form of cutting. Formerly diamonds were unevenly cut in long and square shapes, and such stones, however valuable, cannot compare with the modern round stone in brilliancy or beauty.

The value of a diamond is in increasing ratio as its size increases. For example, a perfect diamond of one carat being worth $150.00, one of two carats would be worth three times as much; but one of ten carats would be worth fully one hundred and ten times as much. A diamond without flaw or tint of any kind is called a diamond of the *first water*.

There are an immense number of imitations of the diamond and purchasers should avoid taking any risks whatever. It must be borne in mind that Jewelers are always unwilling to appraise the value of stones from outside dealers. Color and brilliancy cannot be carried in the memory; these qualities can only be judged by a side-by-side comparison. We urge our customers not to hesitate at any time to ask us to send gems to any address on approval, for examination and close comparison with the offerings of other dealers similarly submitted. Our selections are made with extreme care, our avenues of purchase are exceptional, and our prices *quality always considered*, are very close to actual cost.

COLORED STONES

THE RUBY.

The most valuable of all corundums; fine rubies in sizes of one carat and over are from 3 to 10 times more valuable than diamonds of similar size and quality. Value is a question,— first of clearness and color, next of size, lastly of perfect formation.

The hue most desired is known as "pigeon's blood" and is the color of arterial blood. Clearness is important; examine a ruby carefully for. clouds or milky spots. Cracks or slight de— fective flaws are of less importance, as perfection in a ruby is rarely found and color and brilliancy are considered more essential.

which later examination proved to be simply spinels.

Rubies are full of the sentiment of the East; they are supposed to preserve the health and spirits of the wearer. The supply of rubies since the days of Solomon has steadily diminished, and a perfect ruby is now exceedingly rare. Among the gems now on exhibition at our warerooms is a genuine ruby, probably of Siamese or Burmese origin, not of great size, but of such perfect form and depth and life of color that it is worthy of a visit from all who care to see what a valuable ruby really is.

THE EMERALD.

One of the most highly prized of gem-stones when transparent and of fine color. It should be of the hue of fresh grass in the spring. It is very rare to find an emerald without a flaw. The stone is very light.in weight, and imitations may usually be detected by the scales. "False Emeralds," so called, is fluor spar (made into vases and ornaments) and is slightly luminous in a dark room.

Our stock of Emeralds is always large, whatever the demand, and we solicit a critical comparison of our prices with those of the leading jewelers.

THE SAPPHIRE.

Exactly the same stone as the ruby, but different in color and less rare; hence less valuable, especially in the larger sizes. When of fine quality it is very nearly as valuable as a diamond of the same size and quality. The choicest shades of color are the blue tints of the cornflower and a rich velvety blue. It is an added advantage if the color is equally brilliant by artificial light. Male sapphires (so called) are the deep-colored stones: light-colored ones are female sapphires.

The prevailing sapphire of commerce is of a bluish hue. The sapphire is found, however, in other shades of color as follows:

Green Sapphire, or Oriental Emerald.

Purple Sapphire, or Oriental Amethyst.

Yellow Sapphire, or Oriental Topaz.

Light Green Sapphires, or Oriental Aquamarine.

Greenish yellow Sapphire, or Oriental Crysolite.

Aurora-red Sapphire, or Oriental Hyacinth.

The name "Oriental" is prefixed to distinguish the corundum from the less valuable mineral of the same color. The color, if a corundum, is usually less strong and deep, but the stone is much more brilliant, rare and valuable.

"Star" sapphires (so-called) are extremely rare; they are so crystalized as to exhibit by reflected light a bright six-pointed star.

THE TURQUOISE.

Color, blue or greenish blue, with a waxy lustre, and opaque. The choicest hue is a clear, deep sky blue. In value it ranks below the ruby, diamond, emerald and sapphire, but it is never-theless highly prized and a most valuable additional color among gems.

The best turquoises are the Ameri-can. There are numerous other varieties, notably the Persian and

Egyptian, but they usually fade in color and turn green from exposure to light.

There are numerous counterfeits in turquoises:—Odontolites are cut from fossil teeth of animals and will yield to a file or to nitric acid; "reconstructed" turquoises will quickly darken in color if put into water; artificially colored turquoises can be tested by a drop of ammonia on the back of the stone which will leave a green spot.

The popularity of the turquoise has recently been greatly heightened by the discovery of new mines in this country which produce a stone of exceptional color which *will not fade under any exposure.* We have some of the finest specimens of these new turquoises now on exhibition at our establishment, and they can safely be trusted to hold their exact color. The great objection hitherto to this jewel has been its liability to change in color, but this difficulty has now been wholly overcome.

THE OPAL.

This stone was formerly believed to confer magical virtues upon its wearer, but a later superstition reversed this. It is easy to trace these beliefs to the nature of the stone, which, being soft, was easily scratched, and then appeared to have lost its color. To-day, however, opals are very highly prized. The finest specimens are those from Hungary and Australia; Spanish-American opals are, as a rule, inferior.

The best known varieties of opals are (1) precious or noble opals (highly valued), showing brilliant changeable

color reflections; (2) fire opals, showing fire-like reflection; (3) common
opals, whose colors are milk white,
bluish white, green, red, etc., but
without any fire or reflection; (4)
semi-opals, very opaque; and (5) hydro-
phanes, transparent under water.

The opal is rapidly gaining a marked
ascendancy in popular favor, and the
demand to-day for good opals cannot
be filled although the mines are
worked to their utmost capacity. As
this little volume goes to press we are
in expectation of an interesting in-
voice of opals. soon to arrive at our
warerooms. Notice of their arrival
will be sent to any of our customers
on request.

THE SPINEL.

Only within the last century has
spinel been discovered to be not a

corundum, and thus many reputed rubies and sapphires have proven to be red and blue spinels.

Spinels are exceedingly close to the very precious gems in appearance. They are of various shades; red spinel is the most valuable color and closely resembles the ruby. Ruby spinels of one carat or larger are rare and valuable. Other colors are blue, green, yellow, brown, black and white, the latter being often confounded with the diamond, though less brilliant. As secondary stones, or in combination, spinels are highly effective. They are only surpassed in hardness, beauty and brilliancy by the diamond and the corundums.

Much may be learned of spinels by a visit to our warerooms and a careful examination of our large stock, comprising nearly all colors in many shades. Sapphirine, rubicelle, and balas ruby are only other names for spinel.

THE GARNET.

This stone is found in many varieties, differing in color, composition and weight. The red varieties are most common, but violet, brown, yellow, green and white garnets are not altogether rare. A carbuncle (so-called), is any garnet cut with a smooth, rounding top.

Bohemian garnets are dark blood-red in color and in the larger sizes very valuable. Demantoides (often falsely sold as olivines), Cape rubies, American rubies, cinnamon stones, and almandines are all varieties of garnets.

THE TOURMALINE.

Of all minerals, this precious stone has the largest alphabet of names and colors; it is always, however, readily distinguished from other gems by its electrical properties when heated. It crystalizes in three, six, and nine-sided prisms, often of great size, and of marvelously beautiful color groupings —as for example, red with a blue or green border, brown with a border of old yellow, and many interesting and more confusing blendings.

Familiar varieties are achroite, colorless; rubellite, pink or red; indicolite, blue; and aphritite (or schorl), black. There are also green (Brazilian emeralds), purple (Brazilian sapphires), and yellowish-green (Ceylon crysolites). Transparent varieties are more highly prized than the opaque stones and the red, blue green and harlequin-colored tourmalines, if really fine, are quite valuable.

THE TOPAZ.

This gem is transparent or nearly so, and yellow (Saxony), white (Siberian), green, (aquamarine), pale blue (Brazilian sapphire), pink (Brazilian ruby), or colorless (slave's diamond). The latter variety when pure and cut in facets, closely counterfeits the diamond; in fact the "Braganza," (the great diamond of Portugal) is supposed to be a white topaz.

False topaz is simply yellow quartz, and lacks in brilliancy. Beryl and crysolite are often used to imitate topaz.

THE AMETHYST.

This stone varies in color from light to dark tones of purple and violet.

The price of amethysts is much influenced by fashion; at times they are exceedingly valuable, but at the present writing fine specimens can be secured through us for very little money.

THE BERYL.

(Emerald, Aquamarine, Cat's-eye, Alexandrite.)

A green beryl is an Emerald; a transparent pale-green or a light sky-blue beryl is an Aquamarine, and a golden-yellow beryl is a Chrysoberyl, which latter class are in their turn divided into Cat's-eyes, Cymophanes, and Alexandrites.

All these are familiar stones and it is always possible to secure fine specimens of them at our establishment. Alexandrites are now very much in demand and good specimens of from one to four carats are very quickly seized; the demand exceeds the supply. Cat's-eyes are very extensively imitated in quartz, but the imitation always lacks the brilliancy and high polish of the genuine. The true Crysoberyl or Oriental Cat's-eye has a bright band of light (usually white) running through the centre; in the finer specimens it is clearly defined and in the centre of the stone. The stone itself may be in shades of yellow, brown, green or black.

All varieties of beryls except emeralds are usually very brilliant by artificial light.

THE MOONSTONE.

This beautiful stone is a clear feldspar, colorless or tinted very slightly, with plays of light resembling the pearl. Large quantities are cut like whole pearls for necklaces or brooches, and are in active demand. Size greatly affects their value, however, and the smaller balls are not at all expensive.

THE PEARL.

The value of a pearl depends upon three things:—first, its form (which in order of value must be round, pear-shaped or exactly oval); secondly, its lustre (or "orient," so-called); and thirdly, the purity of its color (any yellow or gray tinge greatly lowering its value, although pearls of decided colors are rarer and often more valuable than the pure white.)

It is of course assumed that the outer surface must be perfectly smooth, without spots, wrinkles or indentations. A rough, oddly-shaped pearl is called a baroque.

A pearl should have the suggestion of transparency and *must have* the peculiar "orient" or lustre, without which even the finest form and color of pearl has but little value. The "orient" in the pearl exactly corresponds to "brilliancy" in the diamond; without it there is no charm.

Black pearls are the most valuable, then pink and yellow; any of these decided colors in a perfect pearl greatly enhances its cost.

Pearls are steadily increasing in price; they cost now from two and a half to three times as much as they did ten years ago, and there is every indication of a continuance of this advance in price, as the demand increases much faster than the supply. A pearl which could have been bought for $1,000 in 1883 is now easily worth from $2,500 to $3,000.

Much that is interesting may be learned about pearls during a half hour spent in our establishment at 56 West 23d Street, and the object of this book would not be attained if we neglected to say before closing that it will give us pleasure to exhibit many precious stones to any reader of this little volume. We especially desire to emphasize the fact that visitors are always cordially welcome, regardless of any intention to purchase.

THEODORE A. KOHN & SON.

CONCERNING MOUNTINGS.

We make a specialty of odd, rare and interesting mountings. While the intrinsic value of a gem is always independent of its setting, it is never-theless through the setting in a marked degree that its value is revealed. The most intelligent class of purchasers never disregard the element of mounting. There is practically no limit to the number of styles, and the service which we are enabled to render to our customers in this connection is correspondingly large. We will always willingly advise upon the most effective method of mounting any particular stone, and an examination of our stock will offer many additional suggestions.

To those executing their purchases at our establishment we can offer:—

First: The advantage of a choice from one of the most exclusive assortments of precious stones in this city.

Secondly: Accurate and complete information and the benefits of expert guidance in all purchases.

Thirdly: Consistently low prices.

Our avenues of selection are extensive and intending buyers may be assured of finding here at all times a large and exclusive collection, comprising all varieties of precious stones in original and artistic mountings.

Apart from our customers, we welcome strangers who visit our establishment without any intention to purchase. It is a pleasure to exhibit rare stones to those who can appreciate their beauty. No visitor is ever urged to purchase.

THEODORE A. KOHN & SON.

www.ingramcontent.com/pod-product-compliance
Lightning Source LLC
Chambersburg PA
CBHW022343280326
41934CB00006B/761